Young Learner's

HOW TO DRAW

Step by Step

Young Learner Publications®
G-1A Rattan Jyoti, 18 Rajendra Place, New Delhi- 110 008 (INDIA)
Tel: 25750801, 25820556, 25755559 Fax: 91-11-25764396
Website: www.goodwillpublishinghouse.com
E-mail: gph.ylp@goodwillpublishinghouse.com
goodwillpub@gmail.com

© Young Learner Publications®, India

All rights reserved. No part of this publication may be reproduced, stored in a retrieval system or transmitted, in any form or by any means—mechanical, photocopying, recording or otherwise, without prior written permission of Young Learner Publications, India.

Landscapes

In a landscape everything is beautiful in whichever direction you look. It is difficult for a beginner to decide which part of the landscape to draw first or how to compose a landscape. There are several approaches. In this exercise, we shall learn about choosing the subject, landscape composition, Rule of Thirds, using a viewfinder and the Law of Golden Section.
Let's start!

Choosing the subject

The first thing which comes to every beginner's mind is where to start. Magazines, travel brochures and old photograph albums can be a great source of inspiration. Another option is to carry a sketchbook or a digital camera and then go outside and click photographs for reference; or draw and colour on the spot. This is the simplest way to start. But remember, you should have a strong centre of interest or a focal point in your landscape. This is the element which will direct the viewer to all the other elements. You can have secondary elements, but try to keep just one centre of interest. Given below are some landscape subjects.

The first stage of any landscape painting is to select your subject. In this landscape, house is the subject.

The house is the centre of interest and focal point of this landscape. It is very important to hold the viewer's interest.

In this landscape the marked rocks are the subject.

The front rocks are the centre of interest and focal point of this landscape.

Landscape Composition

Composition is one of the most interesting and exciting aspects of landscape painting. All the elements of your painting (sky, water, land, trees, buildings, etc.) should be in perfect harmony and balance with each other in terms of scale, shape, colour, rhythm, pattern, etc. You should look at the landscape from various angles till you find the one that appeals to you. Below are some examples of different landscape compositions.

Carefully look at each part of the landscape. Select your subject. In this landscape, rocks and buildings form an interesting composition to draw.

The building is the centre of interest and focal point of this landscape. This is very important to hold the viewer's interest.

Rule of Thirds

Using only four lines (two vertical and two horizontal), the nine-celled grid defines the Rule of Thirds. The four intersecting points (shown in red bullets) and the lines which have been created have a peculiar importance and impact a person's visual experience.

In the first photograph you can see a desert scene. The dry tree is the main subject, centre of interest and focal point of this landscape. The Rule of Thirds requires you to place your centre of interest on one of these intersecting points. By calling it a sweet spot you can arrange a pleasing composition based on that focal point. In the second photograph, the subject is outside these points. As shown in the third photograph, avoid placing objects directly in the centre of the points. Try keeping objects slightly to one side. This will create a more interesting composition.

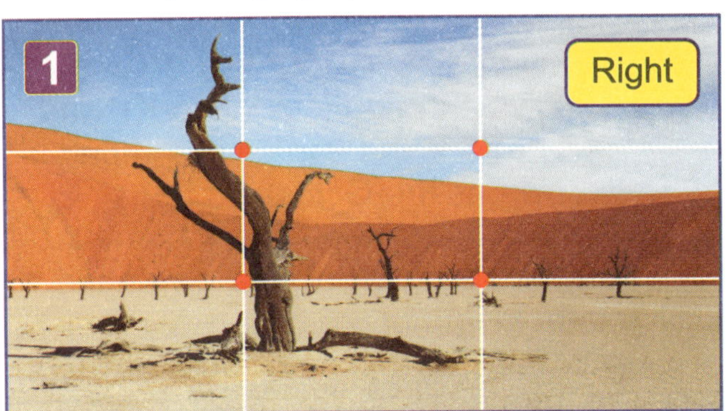

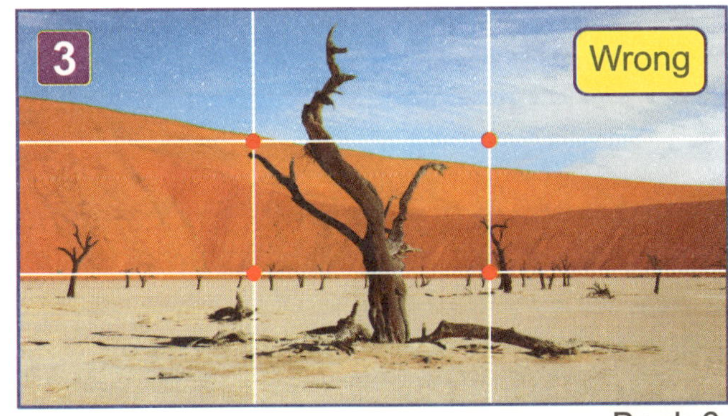

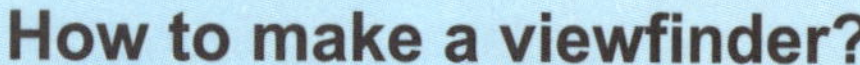

Take a 5" X 4" piece of hard grey cardboard.

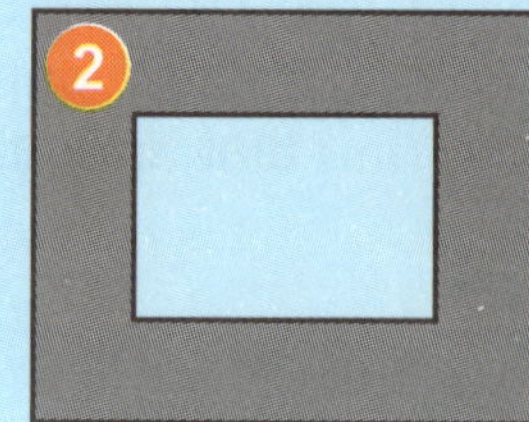

Then, cut out a 3" X 2" piece in the centre.

Take a 3" X 2" transparent plastic sheet. Draw 1 inch grid on plastic sheet with an OHP marker.

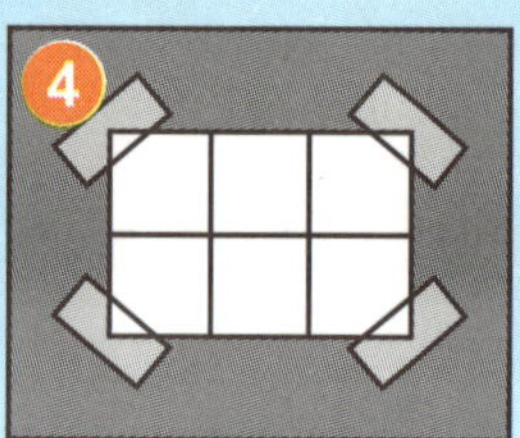

Tape the plastic sheet to the back of the viewfinder.

Using a viewfinder

There are several approaches to composing your painting once you have selected your subject. Using a viewfinder is one simple way. To capture the proportion of your painting surface, look through the viewfinder with one eye while keeping the other eye closed. Move around till you see exactly what you want to draw and then set up your equipment.

Law of Golden Section

The division of a line into two parts such that the ratio of longer length to shorter length is equal to the ratio of total length to longer length is the *Law of Golden Section*. The line XZ has been split in this way: the ratio of YZ to XY and XZ to YZ is the same i.e. 1.6 and is known as the Golden Ratio.

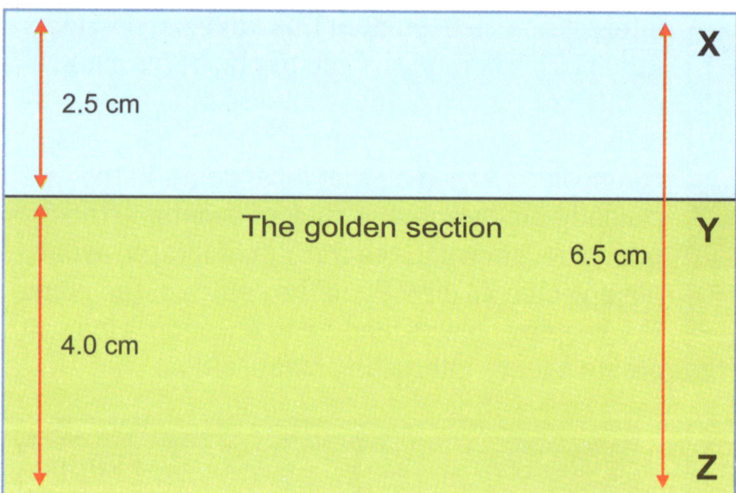

To find the Golden Section in this rectangular landscape, divide the total length of 6.5 by 1.6. We get 4 i.e. the longer length. Subtracting 4 from 6.5 we get 2.5. Therefore, XZ=6.5cm, YZ=4cm, XY=2.5cm are the required lengths.

For teachers and parents: Encourage the children to practise drawing landscapes in their sketchbooks using different subjects and compositions, Rule of Thirds, a viewfinder and the Law of Golden Section. They can use photographs and travel magazines as reference.

Sky and Clouds

A landscape drawing or painting depicts an expanse of natural scenery. The common landscape elements are sky, clouds, mountains, water, valleys, rivers, trees, forests, etc. In this exercise we will learn how to draw and capture the landscape elements by using simple techniques.

Types of sky and clouds

Sky and clouds are very important elements for making a great landscape. The colour of the sky and shape of the clouds sets the mood of any landscape. It also changes the overall feeling of the landscape. You can see some different types of sky and clouds below.

Cumulus clouds are white, puffy clouds that look like puffs of cotton. The base of each cloud is flat and the top is rounded. Cumulus clouds are fairly close to the ground.

Cirrus clouds are feathery and wispy. They are blown by fast winds into long streamers.

Stratus clouds are uniform greyish clouds which evoke a calm feeling. They often cover the entire sky looking like flat sheets of clouds.

Nimbus clouds are dark grey and wet-looking, forming a layer associated with continuously falling rain or snow.

In this lesson we shall learn to draw sky and clouds step by step. Do the shading by hatching technique using colour pencils on cartridge paper. Carefully follow each step to draw the sky and the cumulus clouds. Apply this method on all pencil-shading techniques for drawing other types of clouds in landscapes.

Carefully observe the reference picture of the sky and the clouds and draw the outer shape of the clouds using a light grey pencil.

Start by applying light blue colour to the sky, leaving out the clouds' portion. All shading strokes must be in one single direction.

For showing a curved effect, add more middle tones in top-half portion of the sky. Also, add light and middle tones to the clouds. Remember to keep referring to the original picture.

Finally, add darker pencil strokes to the final details in the sky and clouds.

For teachers and parents: Encourage the children to practise different types of sky and cloud scenes by referring to photographs and travel magazines.

Mountains and Rocks

Mountains and rocks are very important parts of a landscape. Normally, we draw mountains in the background with less detailed shading because they are far away. Sometimes we draw mountains and rocks with highly detailed shading if they are the main subject of our composition. In this exercise we will study different types of mountains and rocks like **dome mountains, volcanic mountains, fault-block mountains, folded mountains** and **plateau mountains.** We will also learn to capture their formations, light and shades.

Types of mountains and rocks

1

Dome mountains are the result of the melting rock pushing its way up under the Earth's crust. If the molten rock breaks through, it forms a volcano, if not, it forms a dome mountain.

2

Volcanic mountains are formed as results of volcanic eruptions. Molten rock deep within the Earth erupts and piles upon the surface. When magma breaks through the Earth's crust it is called lava. It builds a cone of rocks when the ash and lava cool down. Rock and lava pile upon each other.

3

Fault-block mountains are formed when one side of a fault in the Earth's crust slides over another. The cracks in the Earth's crust are the faults. The material from one side gets pushed upward while that from the other side slides downward. After a great amount of intense pressure and over a period of time the uplifted rocks form mountains.

4

Fold mountains are the most common type of mountains. They are formed when two plates collide head on and their edges crumble. The movement of the two plates forces sedimentary rocks upwards into a series of folds.

Plateau Mountains are actually formed by the Earth's internal activity and are revealed by erosion. Plateaus are large flat areas that have been pushed above the sea level by forces within the Earth. Over billions of years, the rivers cut deep into a plateau and make tall mountains. Plateau mountains are usually found near fold mountains.

In this lesson we will learn to draw and shade mountains and rocks using colour pencils. In natural features like mountains, rocks and trees it is very difficult to measure the right proportion. The simplest way to draw in the right proportion is to see the whole shape of mountains and rocks and draw outer forms with very light pencil. Then, draw the detailed shape of each rock and tree on the mountains. Apply this method on all step-by-step pencil-shading techniques for drawing other mountains in landscapes.

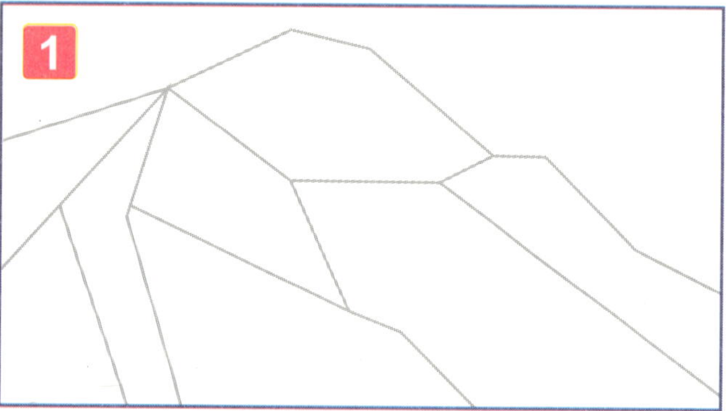

Observe the original picture of the dome mountains for reference. Divide the outer shape of each part into simple shapes using a light grey pencil on the sheet.

Now, fill each shape with detailed outline of the rocks and trees by following the original picture.

Lightly apply blue colour in the sky background. Colour the mountains and trees with grey and green colours respectively. All shading strokes must be in one single direction.

For giving a curved effect to the sky, add more middle tones in the sky area. Also, add highlights and middle tones with light and dark grey pencil colours. This will make the mountain look more realistic. First, complete the middle tones in all parts of the mountain, and then apply the final dark tones. It is a good idea to keep referring to the original image.

While shading with colour pencils, apply the strokes gently and do not press the pencil too hard. It can destroy the grains of the cartridge paper.

Finally, add more dark pencil strokes to the final details in the mountain, rocks and trees. The dome mountain is ready!

For teachers and parents: Encourage the children to practise different types of mountain and rock landscapes by referring to photographs and travel magazines.

Trees and Plants

Trees and plants seem like one of those few objects that are easy to draw. As an artist, you have to draw what you see and not what you know. When sketching outdoors, it is easier to draw a tree which is at a distance, rather than the one which is near. Before you start drawing, analyze the shape and proportion of the tree and study its contours well. This simplifies the problems of detailing, lighting, etc.

Types of trees and plants

Take out some time to just look at and admire nature's beauty. Trees and plants, found in different shapes and sizes, are one of the most beautiful creations of nature. Try not to confuse yourself with the large variety of details that you see in a tree or plant; instead try to convert it into a simple geometrical shape like oval, sphere, cone, etc. The character of a tree or a plant may be determined by its silhouette.

European Larch

In this exercise, we shall learn to draw a realistic European larch tree in a simple manner. First take an overall look and then focus on its details.

1. A European larch tree is shaped like a cone. Draw a very light basic outline of the tree.
2. Draw the trunk and the branches. Too much precision is not needed. Just refer to the original tree every now and then.
3. Draw a contour of the tree crown. It should be narrow and uneven. Keep a lot of empty areas between the branches.
4. Fill the crown of the tree with light green colour and its trunk with dark brown colour.
5. Finally, you can use medium and dark green pencil to draw a few dark (fully shadowed) areas between the branches. Obviously when drawing a tree, we do not draw every single leaf. Foliage should be suggested in relationship to its direction of growth and in a technique which seems best to us to interpret its character and texture. This will improve the contrast of the crown. You can follow these step-by-step instructions for drawing other trees and plants.

Carefully follow all the steps given below to draw different trees. Practise drawing them in your sketchbook using a light pencil and crayons.

1

2

3

4

Chestnut Tree

1

2

3

4

Date Tree

Weeping Willow Tree

Carefully follow all the steps given below to draw different plants. Practise drawing them in your sketchbook using a light pencil and crayons.

Century Plant

Split Leaf Plant

Philodendron Plant

For teachers and parents: Encourage the children to practise different types of trees and plants by referring to garden and nature photographs.

Different Types of Landscape

In the previous pages we have studied different parts of a landscape in a very detailed manner. In this exercise we will combine these elements into a single landscape. We will compose and colour different types of landscapes like mountains, coastlines, forests and deserts. Let's start!

Carefully observe the mountain landscape given below. Colour the same scene in the box given below using colour pencils.

Carefully observe the coastline landscape given below. Colour the same scene in the box given below using colour pencils.

Carefully observe the forest landscape given below. Colour the same scene in the box given below with colour pencils.

Carefully observe the desert landscape given below. Colour the same scene in the box given below using colour pencils.

For teachers and parents: Encourage the children to practise different landscapes using colour pencils in their sketchbooks. They can use photographs and travel magazines for reference.